Robber Flies

Traci Dibble

Look at the fly.

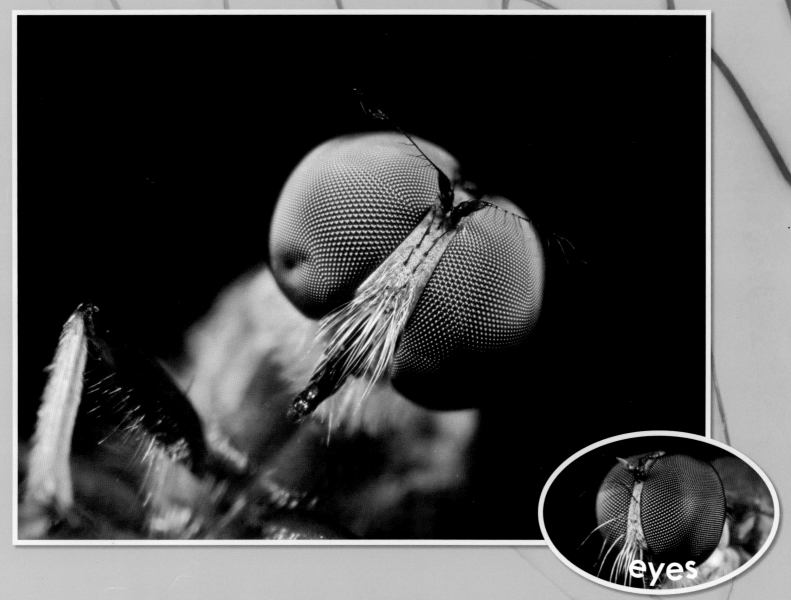

eyes

Look at the eyes.

hair

Look at the hair.

wings

Look at the wings.

legs

Look at the legs.

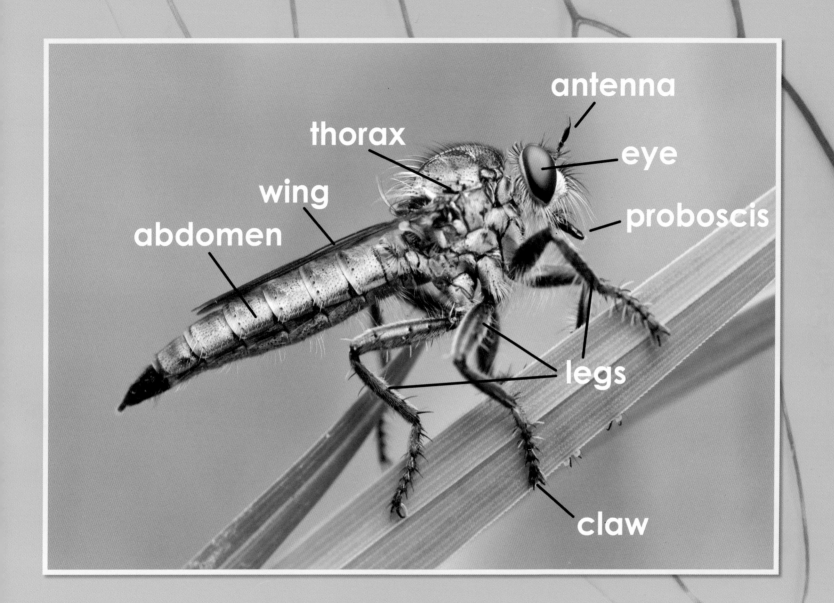

antenna

thorax

eye

wing

proboscis

abdomen

legs

claw

Look at the body.

leaf

Look at the leaf.

stick

Look at the stick.

flower

Look at the flower.

rock

Look at the rock.

ladybug

Look at the ladybug.

fly

Look at the fly.

dragonfly

Look at the dragonfly.

bee

Look at the bee.

I can use the first letter sound to match the word to the picture.

stick

flower

hair

bee

wing